# KATYDIDS

## INSECTS DISCOVERY LIBRARY

Jason Cooper

Rourke Publishing LLC
Vero Beach, Florida 32964

PHOTO CREDITS: Cover, p. 4, 10, 11, 16, 18, 22 (both) © James H. Carmichael; title page, p. 6, 7, 8, 13, 15 © Lynn M. Stone; p. 12, 21 © James P. Rowan

Title page: A katydid steps on a goldenrod flower.

**Library of Congress Cataloging-in-Publication Data**

Cooper, Jason, 1942-
 Katydids / Jason Cooper.
     p. cm. -- (Insects discovery library)
 Includes index.
 Includes bibliographical references.
 ISBN 1-59515-427-2 (hardcover)
 1. Katydids--Juvenile literature. I. Title.
 QL508.T4C66 2006
 595.7'26--dc22
                        2005010971

**Printed in the USA**

CG/CG

Rourke Publishing

www.rourkepublishing.com – sales@rourkepublishing.com
Post Office Box 3328, Vero Beach, FL 32964
1-800-394-7055

# TABLE OF CONTENTS

# Katydids

Katydids are very colorful **insects**. They are also very loud! Male katydids call for mates. Some kinds of katydids sound like they're saying, *katy did*, *katy did*! These sounds gave the katydid its name.

*A colorful katydid perches on an air-plant.*

Many adult katydids have two pair of large wings. Flying katydids don't usually fly far. Katydids often just leap, like grasshoppers. No wonder! Katydids are related to grasshoppers and crickets.

*The grasshopper*

*A katydid at rest folds its wings together.*

# Looking at a Katydid

Katydids have two long antennas on their heads. The antennas may be longer than the katydid's entire body! That body is about as long as your first finger.

*A katydid has long, whip-like antennas.*

A katydid's body may be short or long. The body shape depends upon the kind of katydid. There are hundreds of kinds.

Some katydids look like they wear **armor**. It's really hard skin.

*Katydids come in many colors.*

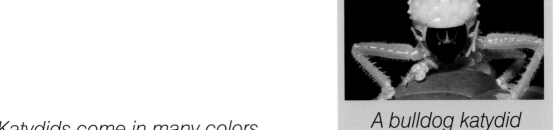

*A bulldog katydid*

Many kinds of katydids hide easily. They are colored like the plants around them. Katydids may look like twigs, leaves, or tree bark.

*This katydid looks like a leaf.*

*A red katydid hides on an orchid flower.*

# Katydid Food

Hidden katydids are not always safe. They are **prey** for many animals. Spiders eat katydids. Lizards, snakes, birds, frogs, and toads also eat them.

*The rough green snake eats katydids.*

14

Most kinds of katydids feed on plants. Katydids
live close to their plant foods, in trees and bushes.
Katydids may also eat dead animals.

*This katydid is eating moss
on tree bark.*

# Being a Katydid

A katydid doesn't have a voice. Katydids rub their wings together to make loud, buzzing sounds.

## Did You Know?
Cone-headed katydids are some of the loudest insects on earth!

*A katydid hears through special patches in its legs.*

# Young Katydids

Katydids hatch from eggs. Baby katydids are called **nymphs**. They look something like adults. But they don't have wings. In time the nymphs change into adult katydids.

*The katydid nymph's wings are just beginning to grow.*

Spines on this
katydid help keep
it safe.

# GLOSSARY

**armor** (AR mur) — a hard coat of metal for soldiers and sometimes a covering for insects

**insects** (IN SEKTZ) — small, boneless animals with six legs

**nymphs** (NIMFZ) — a young stage of life in certain insects, before they become adults

**prey** (PRAY) — any animal caught and eaten by another animal

*The spike makes this a "cone head" or "rhinoceros" katydid.*

# INDEX

## Further Reading

Bishop, Nick. *Katydids*. Richard C. Owen Pubs., 1998

Brennan, Patricia. *Grasshoppers and Their Relatives, Vol. 5*. World Book, 2001

## Websites to Visit

http://www.dnr.state.mn.us/young_naturalists/buggysounds/index.html

http://www.biokids.umich.edu/critters/information/Tettigoniidae.html

## About the Author

Jason Cooper has written many children's books for Rourke Publishing about a variety of topics. Cooper travels widely to gather information for his books.